# What is Nature?

SonLight Education Ministry
United States of America

# A Suggested Daily Schedule

(Adapt this schedule to your family needs.)

| | | |
|---|---|---|
| 5:00 a.m. | | Arise–Personal Worship |

6:00 a.m. — Family Worship and Bible Class–With Father

7:00 a.m. — Breakfast

8:00 a.m. — Practical Arts*–Domestic Activities
  Agriculture
  Industrial Arts
  (especially those related to
  the School Lessons)

10:00 a.m. — School Lessons
(Take a break for some physical exercise
during this time slot.)

12:00 p.m. — Dinner Preparations
(Health class could be included at this time
or a continued story.)

1:00 p.m. — Dinner

2:00 p.m. — Practical Arts* or Fine Arts
(Music and Crafts)
(especially those related to
the School Lessons)

5:00 p.m. — Supper

6:00 p.m. — Family Worship–Father
(Could do History Class)

7:00 p.m. — Personal time with God–Bed Preparation

8:00 p.m. — Bed

*Daily nature walk can be in morning or afternoon.

# The Desire of All Nations

This book is a part of a curriculum that is built upon the life of Christ entitled, "The Desire of All Nations," for grades 2-8. Any of the books in this curriculum can be used by themselves or as an entire program.

## INFORMATION ABOUT THE 2-8 GRADE PROGRAM

## Multi-level

This program is written on a multi-level. That means that each booklet has material for grades 2-8. This is so the whole family in these grades may work from the same books. It is difficult for a busy mother to have 2 or more children and each have a different set of books. Remember, the Bible is written for all ages.

## The Bible—the Primary Textbook

The books in this program are designed to teach the parent and the student how to learn academic subjects by using the Bible as a primary textbook.

## The Desire of Ages

*The Desire of Ages* by Ellen G. White is used as a textbook to go with the Bible. This focuses on the early life of Christ, when He was a child. Children relate best to Christ as a child and youth.

## Lesson Numbers

The big number in the top right corner on the cover of this book is the Lesson Number and corresponds with the chapter number in the book *The Desire of Ages*. For example, Lesson 1 in the school program will go along with chapter 1 in *The Desire of Ages*. Usually each family starts at the beginning with Lesson 1. Most children have not had a true Bible program, therefore they need the foundation built. If there is academic material that they have already covered, they do the Bible part and review then pass quickly on.

## Seven Academic Subjects

There are seven academic subjects in this program—Health, Mathematics, Music, Science–Nature, History/Geography/Prophecy, Language, Voice–Speech.

## Language Program

A good, solid language program is recommended to be used along with the SonLight materials.

The Riggs Institute has a multi-sensory teaching method that accommodates every child's unique learning style. Their program is called *Writing and Spelling Road to Reading and Thinking*. Order by calling (800) 200-4840 or visit www.riggsinst.org. (Disclaimer: SonLight does not endorse the reading books recommended in the Riggs' program.)

Another option which you might find more user friendly and is similar to the Riggs program but from a Christian perspective is *Spell to Write and Read* by Wanda Sanseri. To order, call Wanda Sanseri at (503) 654-2300 or visit https://www.bhibooks.net/swr.html

# "God With Us"
## Lesson 1 – Love

### The following books are those you will need for this lesson.
### All of these can be obtained from www.sonlighteducation.com

**The Rainbow Covenant** – Study the spiritual meaning of colors and make your own rainbow book.

**Health**
*What is Health?*

**Math**
*What is Mathematics?*

**Music**
*What is Music?*

**Science/Nature**
*What is Nature?*

**A Casket** – Coloring book and story. Learn how to treat the gems of the Bible.

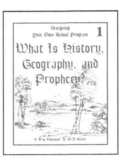

**H/G/P**
*What is History, Geography and Prophecy?*

**Language**
*What is Language?*

**Speech/Voice**
*What is the Voice?*

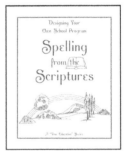

**Spelling from the Scriptures**

**Bible Study** – Learn how to study the Bible and helpful use tools.

**Bible**
*The Desire of all Nations I*
*Teacher Study Guide*

*Student Study Guide*

*Bible Lesson Study Guide*

**Memory Verses**
*The Desire of all Nations I*
*Scripture Songs Book*

*and MP3 files*

**Our Nature Study Book** – Your personal nature journal.

# Outline of "The Desire of all Nations" Lesson 1

| Bible | Health | Math | Music | Nature | H/G/P | Language | Voice |
|---|---|---|---|---|---|---|---|

**Week 1** **Month 1**
**Lesson 1**

**Day 1**

Family Morning Worship

Use these songs during this week, "All Things Bright & Beautiful," "This is My Father's World," and "We Shall Know." Find this music in *Christ in Song* book which is included in these materials under the title "Song Books."

*Covenant Notebook*

(1) Music, Prayer, MV

(2) Read pages 1-2 in the "Covenant Notebook" and discuss.

(3) Sometime during the day take a nature walk looking for rainbows.

(4) Begin finding pictures of complete rainbows to put into the plastic sheets behind the "Rainbows" page. Read and discuss the "Rainbows" page.

---

**READ THIS BEFORE BEGINNING**

Cover the Teacher's Section of each school book before beginning that subject.

It is best to cover only a few concepts at once and understand them well and not run a marathon with a young person's mind. If this outline moves too fast for you SLOW down. Teach one idea and teach it well!

This school program is not a race with time, rather it is an experience with God.

The parents are to represent their Father in Heaven before the children—students.

Together learn about the Character Qualities and help one another in a godly manner to reach the finish line together.

---

**INSTRUCTIONS**

**Day 2**

(1) Music, Prayer, MV

(2) Read page 3 in the "Covenant Notebook" and discuss. (Also use page 7)

Lay out Lesson 1 of the School Program showing the front covers of each book, *What is Health?, What is Mathematics?, What is Music?, What is Nature?, What is H/G/P?, What is Language?, and What is Voice?.* Each book will have a color cover of one of the colors of the rainbow. Place them in order as the rainbow colors

demonstrate in a picture. Refer to page 7 of the *Covenant Notebook* to see what each color means and how it relates to the subject that bears that color.

(Examples:
Health = Christ sacrificed His body on the cross for you.

Mathematics = Deals in numbers saved and lost.

Music = Right music can turn our thoughts from things of this world to Divinity.

Nature = Right growth in character.

H/G/P = The history of obedience and disobedience; geography of lands where the gospel is to be spread; prophecy telling us the future of those keeping the law.

Language and Voice = How God's royal people should write, speak, and act to prepare for His kingdom.

| Bible | Health | Math | Music | Nature | H/G/P | Language | Voice |
|-------|--------|------|-------|--------|-------|----------|-------|

(3) Sometime during the day take a nature walk looking for rainbows.

(4) Begin finding pictures of complete rainbows to put into the plastic sheets behind the "Rainbows" page. Read and discuss the "Rainbows" page.

**Day 3-4**

(1) Music, Prayer, MV

(2) Read pages 4-9 in the "Covenant Notebook" and discuss.

(3) Sometime during the day take a nature walk looking for white items (or the color pages).

(4) Begin finding pictures of white things in nature to put into the plastic sheets behind the "White" page. Read and discuss the "White" page.

**Day 5**

Review what you have learned.

## INSTRUCTIONS

Once the white page is completed then move on to the red page and so forth, always finding things from nature for your pictures. And on your nature walks fine the color you are currently working on. Do not look for man made things! Before going on the nature walk each day, read and discuss the information in the color section.

After day 5, and reviewing only what you have learned to that point, plan only to work on the *Covenant Notebook* one day a week until that book is finished (Use time in the afternoon and not during the regular school hours). However, do not forget to review the *Covenant Notebook* when you deem it necessary, and if you should find a new picture for it, stop and put it into *Covenant Notebook*. It gives you an opportunity to review lessons with the children.

Lesson 12 of Nature in this series is about the rainbow and would be a wonderful time to make a recommitment to God.

This *Covenant Notebook* is to prepare you for the 2-8 School Lessons. On week 2 begin the School Lessons.

vi

| Bible | Health | Math | Music | Nature | H/G/P | Language | Voice |
|---|---|---|---|---|---|---|---|
| Week 2 Lesson 1 | | START THE 2-8 PROGRAM, "The Desire Of All Nations." | | | | | |
| **Day 1**<br>"God With Us"<br>(1) Music ("O Come, O come, Immanuel," "I Love Thee," "Thou didst Leave Thy Throne"), Prayer, MV (Mt 1:21) (2) Read and discuss Ge 3:14-15; 12:1-3. Discuss the Character Quality. | **Day 1**<br>*What Is Health?*<br>(1) Open Bibles and read II Sa 20:9.<br>(2) Read or tell information. Do pages 1-17 or what you can cover. Discuss. | **Day 1**<br>*What Is Math...?*<br>(1) Open Bibles and read Mt 11:29.<br>(2) Read or tell information. Do pages 1-8 or what you can cover. Discuss. | | | | **Day 1**<br>*Writing and Spelling Road to Reading and Thinking (WSRRT)* (1) Do your daily assignments for *WSRRT*.<br><br>If you are still working on this program continue until you finish at least the 2nd teacher's notebook. | |

## INSTRUCTIONS

If you are still using the *Family Bible Lessons* do them for one of your worships each day and use *The Desire of all Nations* for the other worship each day.

These are the items you will need for worship for *The Desire of all Nations* Bible program: Old King James Bible (**NOT** the New King James Bible)
    *"The Desire of all Nations,"* Volume 1, Study Guide for the
        KJV Bible Lessons
    *The Desire of all Nations* Teacher and Student Study Guides #1
        (Chapters from *The Desire of the Ages* Bible text book)
    *The Desire of all Nations* Song Book #1 and CD Music #1
        for Memory Verses
    Christ in Song Song Book #1, 2, 3, 4

These are the items you will need for class time:

    *What is Health?; What is Mathematics?; What is Music?;*
    *What is Nature?; What is H/G/P?; What is Language?; and*
    *What is Voice?.*
    *Our Nature Study Book*    "The Casket" Story & Coloring Book
    *Bible Study*
    Road Map and Route Catalogue

| Bible | Health | Math | Music | Nature | H/G/P | Language | Voice |
|---|---|---|---|---|---|---|---|
| **Day 2** "God With Us" (1) Music ("O Come, O Come, Immanuel," "I Love Thee," "Thou didst Leave Thy Throne"), Prayer, MV (Mt 1:21; Jn 8:28) (2) Read and discuss Gal 3:16; Ge 49:10; De 18:17-19; II Sam 7:12-17. | **Day 2** *What Is Health?* (1) Open Bibles and read I Co 12:23. (2) Read or tell information. Do pages 18-26 or what you can cover. Discuss. | **Day 2** *What Is Math...?* (1) Open Bibles and read Luke 6:38; Is 40:12; Ps 147:4; Is 40:26; Job 28:25. (2) Read or tell information. Do pages 9-22 or what you can cover. Discuss. **END** | | | | **Day 2** *Writing and Spelling Road to Reading and Thinking* (1) Do your daily assignments for *WSRRT*. | |
| **Day 3** "God With Us" (1) Music, Prayer, MV (Mt 1:21; Jn 8:28) (2) Read and discuss Ez 21:25-27; Lu 1:32; Isa 9:6-7. | **Day 3** *What Is Health?* (1) Open Bibles and read Pr 26:2. (2) Read or tell information. Do pages 27-35 or what you can cover. Discuss. | | **Day 3** *What Is Music?* (1) Open Bibles and read Zeph 3:17. (2) Read or tell information. Do pages 1-6 or what you can cover. Discuss. | | | **Day 3** *Writing and Spelling Road to Reading and Thinking* (1) Do your daily assignments for *WSRRT*. | |
| **Day 4** "God With Us" (1) Review what you have already covered. | **Day 4** *What Is Health?* (1) Review pages 1-35. | **Day 4** *What Is Math...?* (1) Review. | **Day 4** *What Is Music?* (1) Open Bibles and read Re 14:2-3. (2) Read or tell information. Do pages 7-17 or what you can cover. Discuss. | | | **Day 4** *Writing and Spelling Road to Reading and Thinking* (1) Do your daily assignments for *WSRRT*. | |
| **Day 5** | **Day 5** | **Day 5** | **Day 5** | | | **Day 5** Review | |

Find practical applications from your textbooks you have thus far used this week. You will find them listed under "**Reinforce**." Choose and use today.

| Bible | Health | Math | Music | Nature | H/G/P | Language | Voice |
|-------|--------|------|-------|--------|-------|----------|-------|
| **Week 3**<br>**Lesson 1**<br>**Day 1**<br>"God With Us"<br>(1) Music, Prayer, MV (Mt 1:21; Jn 8:28)<br>(2) Read and discuss Ps 45:1-8; 72:1-11; Is 53. | **Day 1**<br>*What Is Health?*<br>(1) Open Bibles and read James 5:14.<br>(2) Read or tell information. Do pages 36-39 or what you can cover. Discuss. | | **Day 1**<br>*What Is Music?*<br>(1) Open Bibles and read I Ki 19:12.<br>(2) Read or tell information. Do pages 18-30 or what you can cover. Discuss. | | | **Day 1**<br>*Writing and Spelling Road to Reading and Thinking*<br>(1) Do your daily assignments for *WSRRT.* | |
| **Day 2**<br>"God With Us"<br>(1) Music, Prayer, MV (Mt 1:21; Jn 8:28; Jn 8:50)<br>(2) Read and discuss Zec 12:10; Jn 14:9; Mt 1:23; Jn 1:1-4. | **Day 2**<br>*What Is Health?*<br>(1) Open Bibles and read De 34:7.<br>(2) Read or tell information. Do pages 40-44 or what you can cover. Discuss. | | **Day 2**<br>*What Is Music?*<br>(1) Open Bibles and read I Chr 13:8.<br>(2) Read or tell information. Do pages 31-52 or what you can cover. Discuss.<br>END | | | **Day 2**<br>*Writing and Spelling Road to Reading and Thinking*<br>(1) Do your daily assignments for *WSRRT.* | |
| **Day 3**<br>"God With Us"<br>(1) Music, Prayer, MV (Mt 1:21; Jn 8:28; Jn 8:50; Phil 2:5-11)<br>(2) Read and discuss *The Desire of Ages* 19-20:0. | **Day 3**<br>*What Is Health?*<br>(1) Open Bibles and read Ez 33:11.<br>(2) Read or tell information. Do pages 45-53 or what you can cover. Discuss. | | | **Day 3**<br>*What Is Nature?*<br>(1) Open Bibles and read Ro 13:10.<br>(2) Read or tell information. Do pages 1-11 or what you can cover. Discuss. | | **Day 3**<br>*Writing and Spelling Road to Reading and Thinking*<br>(1) Do your daily assignments for *WSRRT.* | |

| Bible | Health | Math | Music | Nature | H/G/P | Language | Voice |
|---|---|---|---|---|---|---|---|
| **Day 4** "God With Us" (1) Music, Prayer, MV (Mt 1:21; Jn 8:28; Jn 8:50; Phil 2:5-11) (2) Read and discuss *The Desire of Ages* 20:2-21:0. | **Day 4** *What Is Health?* (1) Open Bibles and read De 7:15; De 32:46; and Pr 4:20, 22. (2) Read or tell information. Do pages 54-60 or what you can cover. Discuss. | | | **Day 4** *What Is Nature?* (1) Open Bibles and read Ps 40:5; Ps 111:4. (2) Read or tell information. Do pages 12-17 or what you can cover. Discuss. | | **Day 4** *Writing and Spelling Road to Reading and Thinking* (1) Do your daily assignments for *WSRRT.* | |
| **Day 5** "God With Us" (1) Review. | **Day 5** *What Is Health?* (1) Review pages 1-60. | **Day 5** *What Is Math...?* (1) Review. | **Day 5** *What Is Music?* (1) Review. | **Day 5** *What Is Nature?* (1) Review pages 1-17. | | **Day 5** *Writing and Spelling Road to Reading and Thinking* (1) Do your daily assignments for *WSRRT.* | |
| **Week 4 Lesson 1** | | | | | | | |
| **Day 1** "God With Us" (1) Music, Prayer, MV (Mt 1:21; Jn 8:28; Jn 8:50; Phil 2:5-11) (2) Read and discuss *The Desire of Ages* 21:1-2. | **Day 1** *What Is Health?* (1) Open Bibles and read De 7:15; De 32:46; and Pr 4:20, 22. (2) Read the story. Do pages 61-80. Discuss. | | | **Day 1** *What Is Nature?* (1) Open Bibles and read Job 12:7-8. (2) Read or tell information. Do pages 18-23 or what you can cover. Discuss. | | **Day 1** *Writing and Spelling Road to Reading and Thinking* (1) Do your daily assignments for *WSRRT.* | |
| **Day 2** "God With Us" (1) Music, Prayer, MV (Mt 1:21; Jn 8:28; Jn 8:50; Phil 2:5-11) (2) Read and discuss *The Desire of Ages* 21:3-22:1. | **Day 2** *What Is Health* (1) Open Bibles and review De 7:15; De 32:46; and Pr 4:20, 22. (2) Do pages 81-86. Discuss. **END** | | | **Day 2** *What Is Nature?* (1) Open Bibles and read Ps 143:5. (2) Read or tell information. Do pages 24-30 or what you can cover. **END** | | **Day 2** *WSRRT* (1) Do your daily assignments for *WSRRT.* Continue the *WSRRT* but add the Language lessons in whenever it is time to do them. **This will not be repeated.** | |

| Bible | Health | Math | Music | Nature | H/G/P | Language | Voice |
|---|---|---|---|---|---|---|---|
| **Day 3** "God With Us" (1) Music, Prayer, MV (Mt 1:21; Jn 8:28; Jn 8:50; Phil 2:5-11) (2) Read and discuss *The Desire of Ages* 21:3-22:3. | | | | | **Day 3** *What Is H/G/P?* (1) Open Bibles and read He 1:10. (2) Read or tell information. Do pages 1-6 or what you can cover. Discuss. Choose a good mission book to begin reading as a family. | **Day 3** *What Is Language?* (1) Open Bibles and read Col 3:16. (2) Read or tell information. Do pages 1-10 or what you can cover + *WSRRT*. Discuss. | |
| **Day 4** "God With Us" (1) Music, Prayer, MV (Mt 1:21; Jn 8:28; Jn 8:50; Phil 2:5-11) (2) Read and discuss *The Desire of Ages* 22:4-24:1. | | | | | **Day 4** *What Is H/G/P?* (1) Open Bibles and read Ps 119:105 & He 13:1. (2) Read or tell information. Do pages 7-14. Discuss. | **Day 4** *What Is Language?* (1) Open Bibles and read Pr 25:11. (2) Read or tell information. Do pages 11-17 + *WSRRT*. Discuss. | **Day 4** *What Is Voice?* (1) Open Bibles and read Ps 105:2. (2) Read or tell information. Do pages 1-4 Discuss. |
| **Day 5** "God With Us" (1) Review. (2) Read and discuss *The Desire of Ages* 24:2-26:3. | **Day 5** *What Is Health?* (1) Review | **Day 5** *What Is Math...?* (1) Review. | **Day 5** *What Is Music?* (1) Review. | **Day 5** *What Is Nature?* (1) Review. | **Day 5** *What Is H/G/P?* (1) Review pages 1-14. | **Day 5** *What Is Language?* (1) Review pages 1-17. | **Day 5** *What Is Voice?* (1) Review pages 1-4. |
| **Week 1 (5) Lesson 1** | Month 2 | | | | | | |
| **Day 1** "God With Us" (1) Music, Prayer, MV. (2) Read and discuss *The Desire of Ages* 24:2-26:3. | | If there is any information that the student should know and does not—REVIEW. | | | **Day 1** *What Is H/G/P?* (1) Open Bibles and read Jer 10:12. (2) Read or tell information. Do pages 15-25Aa or what you can cover. Discuss. | Do your daily assignments for *WSRRT*. **Day 1** *What Is Language?* (1) Open Bibles and read Jn 1:1. (2) Read or tell information. Do pages 18-22 or what you can cover. Discuss. **END** | **Day 1** *What Is Voice?* (1) Open Bibles and read Ps 32:2. (2) Read or tell information. Do pages 5-8. Discuss. **END** |

| Bible | Health | Math | Music | Nature | H/G/P | Language | Voice |
|---|---|---|---|---|---|---|---|
| **Day 2** "God With Us" (1) Music, Prayer, MV. (2) Expand or review any part of the lesson. (Could use section about William Miller in H/G/P.) | | | | | **Day 2** *What Is H/G/P?* (1) Open Bibles and read II Pe 1:21. (2) Read or tell information. Do pages 26-47 or what you can cover. Discuss. (Story about "William Miller" may take longer.) | **Day 2** *Writing and Spelling Road to Reading and Thinking* (1) Do your daily assignments for *WSRRT*. | **Day 2** *What Is Voice?* (1) Review |
| **Day 3** "God With Us" (1) Music, Prayer, MV. (2) Expand or review any part of the lesson. (Could use the section in H/G/P, "The Schools of the Prophets.") | | | | | **Day 3** *What Is H/G/P?* (1) Open Bibles and read Ja 3:17 & Pr 9:10. (2) Read or tell information. Do pages 48-65 or what you can cover. Discuss. | **Day 3** *Writing and Spelling Road to Reading and Thinking* (1) Do your daily assignments for *WSRRT*. | |
| **Day 4** "God With Us" (1) Music, Prayer, MV. (2) Expand or review any part of the lesson. (Could explain why the Apocrypha books are not included in Bible.) END | | | | | **Day 4** *What Is H/G/P?* (1) Open Bibles and read Ex 17:14 & Ge 5:22. (2) Read or tell information. Do pages 66-78 or what you can cover. Discuss. END | **Day 4** *Writing and Spelling Road to Reading and Thinking* (1) Do your daily assignments for *WSRRT*. | **Day 4-5** Use this time to review anything from lesson 1. |

On day 5 review any subject in Lesson 1 that needs a better understanding.

Continue the process with Lesson 2. See the *Road Map and Route Catalogue*.

**Week 2** | **Month 2**
**Lesson 2**
**Day 1**
"The Chosen People" (1) Music, Prayer, MV. (2) Read and discuss.

# Nature Instructions

1. Nature walks are important each week. Learn the joy of discovering insights into God's character as you study His creation.

2. In Lesson Nine of the training course, *Ten Principles of True Education*, under the section, "Academics from the Bible," you will find more information on teaching nature.

3. Nature walks are taken associated with language, Mathematics, Health, History/Geography/Prophecy, and Music

4. Our Nature Study Book is to be used to help parents and teachers have a guide about how to take a nature walk.

# Table of Contents

**Teacher Section**                                            **Pages 1-16**

**Student Section**                                         **Pages 1-30**

**Research**

God's First Book — Page 1
"What I Love" – Poem — Page 2
"A Naturalist's Boyhood Home" – Story — Page 3
Review — Page 10

**Research**

Wonderful Works — Page 12
The Adaptation of Nature to the Human Mind — Page 13
Understanding Nature — Page 14
Before the Fall — Page 15
After the Fall — Page 16
Nature Is a Key — Page 17
Reinforce – Treasure Hunt! — Page 17
"God's Treasuries" – Article — Page 18
Subjects — Page 20
Review — Page 21
"God's Thoughts" – Poem — Page 22
"What Is Nature?" – Activity — Page 23
"God Seen in All His Works" – Story — Page 24
"There Is a God" – Poem — Page 26
Mark Your Bible – "Nature" — Page 27
Remind — Page 28
Reinforce — Page 29
Ruminate — Page 30

# Harmony

"Since the book of nature
and the book of revelation
bear the impress
of the same master mind,
they cannot but speak in **harmony**.
By different methods,
and in different languages,
they witness to the same great truths.
Science is ever discovering new wonders;
but she brings from her research
nothing that, rightly understood,
conflicts with divine revelation.
The book of nature and the written word
shed light upon each other.
They make us acquainted with God
by teaching us something
of the laws through with He works."

—*Education* 128

# Teacher Section

"I will meditate also of all thy work,
and talk of thy doings."
Psalm 77:12

# INSTRUCTIONS
## for the Teacher

## Step 1

Study the Bible Lesson and begin to memorize the Memory Verses. Familiarize yourself with the Character Quality. The student can answer the Bible Review Questions. See page 6. Use the Steps in Bible Study.

## Bible Lesson

**"God With Us"** – Genesis 3:14-15; 12:1-3; Galatians 3:16; Genesis 49:10; Deuteronomy 18:17-19; II Samuel 7:12-17; Ezekiel 21:25-27; Luke 1:32; Isaiah 9:6-7; Psalm 45:1-8; 72:1-11; Isaiah 53; Zechariah 12:10; John 14:9; Matthew 1:23; John 1:1-4

## Memory Verses

Matthew 1:23; Matthew 1:20-21; John 8:28; 6:57; 7:18; 8:50; Philippians 2:5-11

## Character Quality

**Love** – an affection of the mind excited by beauty and worth of any kind, or by the qualities of an object; charity.

Antonyms – hate, detestableness, abomination, loathing, scorn, disdainfulness, selfishness

**Character Quality Verse**

I Corinthians 13:4-7 – *"**Charity** suffereth long, and is kind; **charity** envieth not; **charity** vaunteth not itself, is not puffed up,*

*"Doth not behave itself unseemly, seeketh not her own, is not easily provoked, thinketh no evil;*

*"Rejoiceth not in iniquity, but rejoiceth in the truth;*

*"Beareth all things, believeth all things, hopeth all things, endureth all things."*

## Step 2

**Understand How To/And**

A. Do the spelling cards so the student can begin to build his own spiritual dictionary.

B. Mark the Bible.

C. Evaluate Your Student's Character in relation to the character quality of **love**.

D. Familiarize Yourself with the Things of Nature. Notice the Projects.

E. Review the Scripture References for "Nature."

F. Notice the Answer Key.

# A. Spelling Cards Spelling Lists

| **Nature Words Place I - II - III** | **Bible Words** |
|---|---|
| audible | blessing |
| **charity** | bruise |
| evolution | Emmanuel |
| handwriting | enmity |
| interpret | forever |
| interpreter | head |
| **love** | heel |
| misreading | Judah |
| mysterious | kingdom |
| nature | lawgiver |
| naturalist | peace |
| visible | Prophet |
| | scepter |
| | seed |
| **See the booklet** | Shiloh |
| *Spelling From* | throne |
| *the Scripture* | woman |
| **for instructions.** | |

# B. How to Mark the Bible

1. Copy the list of Bible texts in the back of the Bible on an empty page as a guide.

2. Go to the first text in the Bible and copy the next text beside it. Go to the next one and repeat the process until they are all chain referenced.

3. Have the student present the study to family and/or friends.

4. In each student lesson there is one or more sections that have a Bible marking study on the subject studied. (See the student section, page 27.)

# C. Evaluate Your Student's Character

This section is for the purpose of helping the teacher know how to encourage the student in becoming more **loving.**

See page 7.

---

**Place I = Grades 2-3-4**
**Place II = Grades 4-5-6**
**Place III = Grades 6-7-8**

---

# D. Familiarize Yourself With the Things of Nature – Notice the Projects

## Projects

1. As a family take a nature walk each day. It can remind you how the Creator walked with Adam and Eve in the cool of the day while teaching them lessons from nature.

2. For one nature walk divide the following list of nature study subjects up into lists between teacher and each student. Each person will describe the item as it reveals the character quality of God—**love**. Also describe hatred, the character quality of Satan, in the same item (as it has been perverted from God's original design). Find and read **love** verses from the Bible (example— I John 4:14).

List of Nature Study Subjects

| | | |
|---|---|---|
| animal | astronomy | bird |
| botany | butterfly | desert |
| Earth | fish | flower |
| forest | fruit | garden |
| geology | insect | leaf |
| mountain | ocean | plant |
| rock | season | seed |
| tree | vegetable | volcano |
| water | weather | zoology |

You may make your own list of subjects or add more subjects to this list.

**An example of the above activity:** flowers—God gave the flowers as a bouquet of **love** to us in beauty, scent, and variety. Sin (Satan) has brought death and this beautiful symbol of **love** fades and dies. Discuss this together as a family

Discuss how nature reveals both **love** and hatred. God helps us better understand Him as we view the visible reflections of His **love**.

3. Choose someone who is seldom noticed and prepare a nature bouquet and present to them in **love**.

4. Sing the hymns, "This Is My Father's World" and "All Things Bright and Beautiful."

# E. Review the Scripture References for "Nature"

Teacher, read through this section before working on the lesson with the student.

See page 10.

# F. Notice the Answer Key

The Answer Key for the student book is found on page 8.

**Jesus Came From Heaven**

**Read the Lesson Aim.**

## Lesson Aim

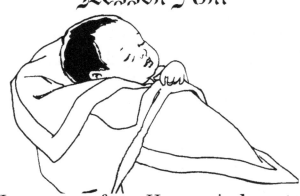

Jesus came from Heaven in **love** to take the human nature of man. All of nature teaches the character, or nature, of God. Satan's character, or nature, is the opposite of Jesus'. **Love** is the motivating power of God. Hatred is the motivating power of Satan. Satan has tried to spoil God's wonderful creation, but still there is much that is lovely. As we behold the beautiful and grand in nature, our hearts respond in **love** and gratitude to the Giver.

God designed the plants and animals, the earth, and all creation to teach us about Himself. As it is written, *"The invisible things of him from the creation of the world are clearly seen, being understood by the things that are made, even his eternal power and Godhead"* (Romans 1:20).

## Step 4

**Prepare to begin
the Nature Lesson.**

## To Begin the Nature Lesson

Visit a beautiful garden, go to a zoo, or go for an outing in the mountains, or desert. If none of these projects can be done, look at a picture book with pictures of nature.

## Step 5

**Begin the Nature Lesson. Cover only what can be understood by your student. Make the lessons a family project by all being involved in part or all of the lesson. These lessons are designed for the whole family.**

## Steps in Bible Study

1. Prayer

2. Read the verses/meditate/memorize.

3. Look up key words in *Strong's Concordance* and find their meaning in the Hebrew or Greek dictionary in the back of that book.

4. Cross-reference (marginal reference) with other Bible texts. An excellent study tool is *"The Treasury of Scripture Knowledge."*

5. Use Bible custom books for more information on the times.

6. Write a summary of what you have learned from those verses.

7. Mark key thoughts in the margin of your Bible.

8. Share your study with others to reinforce the lessons you have learned.

# Review Questions

1. What were the circumstances under which the first promise of a Redeemer was given? (Genesis 3:14-15)

2. What promise was made to Abraham, and what did it mean? (Genesis 12:1-3; Galatians 3:16)

3. Through what tribe of Israel was the Messiah to come? (Genesis 49:10)

4. What promise was given through Moses? (Deuteronomy 18:17-19)

5. Through whom was the permanence of David's kingdom assured? (II Samuel 7:12-17; Ezekiel 21:25-27; Luke 1:32)

6. What exalted ideas concerning the Messiah were made prominent? (Isaiah 9:6-7; Psalm 45:1-8; 72:1-11)

7. What also was foretold of His relation to sin? (Isaiah 53; Zechariah 12:10)

8. What is the significance of the name which is applies to Christ? (John 1:29; Matthew 1:23)

9. What important facts are stated of Him in John 1:1-4
   a.
   b.
   c.

10. As part of the great scheme of human redemption, what did the Word become? What is the meaning of the words *"made flesh"*? (John 1:14)

## Notes

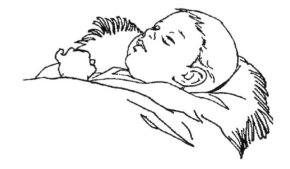

# Evaluating Your Child's Character

Check the appropriate box for your student's level of development, or your own, as the case may be.

Maturing Nicely (MN), Needs Improvement (NI), Poorly Developed (PD), Absent (A)

## Love

1. *"**Charity** suffereth long, and is kind"* (I Corinthians 13:4). Does my child show a maturity of **love** that enables them to be kind while suffering from hunger, tiredness, or discomfort?

**MN   NI   PD   A**
❏    ❏    ❏    ❏

2. When the child encounters people with characters deficiencies, is the child's reaction one of **loving** pity and concern instead of condemnation?

**MN   NI   PD   A**
❏    ❏    ❏    ❏

3. Does your child seem to **love** God more as a result of studying the material contained in the Bible?

**MN   NI   PD   A**
❏    ❏    ❏    ❏

4. *"**Charity** vaunteth not itself, is not puffed up."* Does the child refrain from comparing himself with others? Does he make comments like "I can read better than _____ ."

**MN   NI   PD   A**
❏    ❏    ❏    ❏

5. *"**Charity**...seeketh not her own."* Is the child willing for others to have the best or the most of desirable things?

**MN   NI   PD   A**
❏    ❏    ❏    ❏

6. *"**Love** your enemies."* Does the child initiate reconciliation with or do kind things for those who have hard feelings toward him or who have treated him unfairly?

**MN   NI   PD   A**
❏    ❏    ❏    ❏

7. *"**Charity** shall cover a multitude of sins."* Is the child eager to tell you about the failures of others or do they **lovingly** shield others from exposure where possible to do so with integrity?

**MN   NI   PD   A**
❏    ❏    ❏    ❏

8. *"**Charity**...thinketh no evil."* Is the child unsuspecting, ever placing the most favorable construction upon the motives and acts of others?

**MN   NI   PD   A**
❏    ❏    ❏    ❏

# Answer Sheet

**Page 10**

1.
naturalists = people who study nature

haw = a direction to turn to the left

gee = a direction to turn to the right

section = a piece of land one square mile in area

carex = a plant such as rush

sparsely = thinly scattered; set or planted here and there

prime = having the highest quality of value

gouges = a round hollow chisels, used to cut holes, channels, or grooves in wood or stone

Yankee = a corrupt pronunciation of the word English by the native Indians of America

tranquil = quiet, calm, undisturbed, peaceful, not agitated

**Page 10 continued**

hylas = tree frogs

elocution = act of public speaking

**Page 11**

2.
Blue jay – 3, 8, 10

Woodpecker – 5

Hen hawk – 2, 10

Kingbird – 6

Whippoorwill – 4

Bullbat – 1, 7

3. Book of Nature; Nature is the picture book reflecting the character of God, while the Bible is a book of precious words telling about God's character.

**Page 13**

Student, answer.

**Page 17**

Teacher, check.

# Answer Sheet

**Page 21**

1. Teacher, check.

2. the Book of Nature
It has endless lessons to teach us about the self-sacrificing **love** of our precious Saviour.

3. Nature is the *"wonderful works"* of God.

4. yes

5. prayer, Holy Spirit

6. spiritual vision

7. treasure-house of the Word

8. nature

9. endless lessons, teach, **love**

## Notes

# Scripture References
## Nature

### The Works of God

**Psalm 104:24** – *"O Lord, how manifold are thy works! in wisdom hast thou made them all: the earth is full of thy riches."*

**Psalm 40:5** – *"Many, O Lord my God, are thy wonderful works which thou hast done, and thy thoughts which are to usward."*

**Psalm 92:4-5** – *"For thou, Lord, hast made me glad through thy work: I will triumph in the works of thy hands.*

*"O Lord, how great are thy works! and thy thoughts are very deep."*

**Psalm 111:2-4, 6** – *"The works of the Lord are great, sought out of all them that have pleasure therein.*

*"His work is honourable and glorious: and his righteousness endureth for ever.*

*"He hath made his wonderful works to be remembered...*

*"He hath shewed his people the power of his works, that he may give them the heritage of the heathen."*

**Psalm 19:1-4** – *"The heavens declare the glory of God; and the firmament sheweth his handywork.*

*"Day unto day uttereth speech, and night unto night sheweth knowledge.*

*"There is no speech nor language, where their voice is not heard.*

*"Their line is gone out through all the earth, and their words to the end of the world."*

**Proverbs 3:19** – *"The Lord by wisdom hath founded the earth; by understanding hath he established the heavens."*

### To Be Studied

**Psalm 143:5** – *"I meditate on all thy works; I muse on the work of thy hands."*

**Matthew 6:28** – *"Consider the lilies of the field, how they grow."*

**Job 12:7-8** – *"But ask now the beasts, and they shall teach thee; and the fowls of the air, and they shall tell thee:*

*"Or speak to the earth and it shall teach thee: and the fishes of the sea shall declare unto thee."*

# Understood With God's Help

## Example—The Case of Solomon

**I Kings 3:5-12** – *"In Gibeon the Lord appeared to Solomon in a dream by night: and God said, Ask what I shall give thee.*

*"And Solomon said, Thou hast shewed unto thy servant David my father great mercy, according as he walked before thee in truth, and in righteousness, and in uprightness of heart with thee; and thou hast kept for him this great kindness, that thou hast given him a son to sit on his throne, as it is this day.*

*"And now, O Lord my God, thou hast made thy servant king instead of David my father: and I am but a little child: I know not how to go out or come in.*

*"And thy servant is in the midst of thy people which thou hast chosen, a great people, that cannot be numbered nor counted for multitude.*

*"Give therefore thy servant an **understanding heart** to judge thy people that I may **discern** between*

*good and bad: for who is able to judge this thy so great a people?*

*"And the speech pleased the Lord, that Solomon had asked this thing.*

*"And God said unto him, Because thou hast asked this thing, and hast not asked for thyself long life; neither hast asked riches for thyself, nor hast asked the life of thine enemies; but hast asked for thyself **understanding to discern** judgment;*

*"Behold, I have done according to thy words: lo, I have given thee a wise and an understanding heart; so that there was none like thee before thee, neither after thee shall any arise like unto thee."*

**I Kings 4:29-34** – *"And **God gave Solomon wisdom and understanding exceeding much**, and largeness of heart, even as the sand that is on the sea shore.*

*"And Solomon's wisdom excelled the wisdom of all the children of the east country, and all the wisdom of Egypt.*

*"For he was wiser than all men… and his fame was in all nations round about.*

*"And he spake three thousand proverbs: and his songs were a thousand and five.*

**"And he spake of trees, from the cedar tree that is in Lebanon even unto the hyssop that springeth out of the wall: he spake also of beasts, and of fowl, and of creeping things, and of fishes.**

**"And there came of all people to hear the wisdom of Solomon, from all kings of the earth, which had heard of his wisdom."**

# Nature

*Education* 128 – "Since the book of nature and the book of revelation bear the impress of the same master mind, they cannot but speak in harmony. By different methods, and in different languages, they witness to the same great truths. Science is ever discovering new wonders; but she brings from her research nothing that, rightly understood, conflicts with divine revelation. The book of nature and the written Word shed light upon each other. They make us acquainted with God by teaching us something of the laws through which He works."

*7 Bible Commentary* 916 – "Ignorance may seek to support false views of God by appeals to science; but the book of nature and the written Word do not disagree; each sheds light on the other. Rightly understood, they make us acquainted with God and His character by teaching us something of the wise and beneficent laws through which He works."

*My Life Today* 294 – "God has surrounded us with nature's beautiful scenery to attract and interest the mind. It is His design that we should associate the glories of nature with His character. If we faithfully study the book of nature, we shall find it a fruitful source for contemplating the infinite love and power of God…The heart is quickened, and throbs with new and deeper love, mingled with awe and reverence, as we contemplate God in nature."

*Education* 16-17 – "Adam and Eve received knowledge through direct communion with God; and they learned of Him through His works. All created things, in their original perfection, were an expression of the thought of God. To Adam and Eve nature was teeming with divine wisdom. But by transgression man was cut off from learning of God through direct communion and, to a great degree, through His works. The earth, marred and defiled by sin, reflects but dimly the Creator's glory. It is true that His object lessons are not obliterated. Upon every page of the great volume of His created works may still be traced His handwriting.

"Nature still speaks of her Creator. Yet these revelations are partial and imperfect. And in our fallen state, with weakened powers and restricted vision, we are incapable of interpreting aright. We need the fuller revelation of Himself that God has given in His written word."

*Patriarchs and Prophets* 48 – "God designs that the Sabbath shall direct the minds of men to His created works. Nature speaks to their senses, declaring that there is a living God, the Creator, the Supreme Ruler of all."

*Christ's Object Lessons* 125-126 – "The great storehouse of truth is the Word of God—the written Word, the book of nature, and the book of experience in God's dealing with human life. Here are the treasures from which Christ's workers are to draw. In the search after truth they are to depend upon God, not upon human intelligences, the great men whose wisdom is foolishness with God. Through His own appointed channels the Lord will impart a knowledge of Himself to every seeker.

"If the follower of Christ will believe His word and practice it, there is no science in the natural world that he will not be able to grasp and appreciate. There is nothing but that will furnish him means for imparting the truth to others. Natural science is a treasure house of knowledge from which every student in the school of Christ may draw. As we contemplate the beauty of nature, as we study its lessons in the cultivation of the soil, in the growth of the trees, in all the wonders of earth and sea and sky, there will come to us a new perception of truth. And they mysteries connected with God's dealings with men, the depths of His wisdom and judgment as seen in human life—these are found to be a storehouse rich in treasure."

*Christ's Object Lessons* 24 – "The book of nature is a great lesson book, which in connection with the Scriptures we are to use in teaching others of His character, and guiding lost sheep back to the fold of God. As the works of God are studies, the Holy Spirit flashes conviction into the mind. It is not the conviction that logical reasoning produces; but unless the mind has become too dark to know God, the eye too dim to see Him, the ear too dull to hear His voice, a deeper meaning is grasped, and the sublime, spiritual truths of the written Word are impressed on the heart. In these lessons direct from nature, there is a simplicity and purity that makes them of the highest value. All need the teaching to be derived from this source. In itself the beauty of nature leads the soul away from sin and worldly attractions, and toward purity, peace, and God."

*Counsels to Teachers* 376 – "There are great possibilities in the human understanding when connected with the True Teacher, who in His presentation of the things of the natural world revealed truth in its practical bearings. God works all unseen upon the human heart; for without the divine power operating upon the understanding, the mind of man cannot grasp the sentiments of elevating, ennobling truth. It cannot read the book of nature, nor can it understand the simplicity of godliness found therein. When the human mind is freed from perverting influences, it can receive the lessons of Christ. But no man can understand the true science of education, only as God in His wisdom shall through the Holy Spirit sanctify his observation."

*Counsels to Teachers* 185 –"While the Bible should hold the first place in the education of children and youth, the book of nature is next in importance."

*5 Bible Commentary* 1087 –"God's love is represented by the beautiful things of His creation. These things mean more than many suppose."

*Child Guidance* 45 – "The whole natural world is designed to be an interpreter of the things of God."

*Child Guidance* 46 – "Where once was written only the character of God, the knowledge of good, was now written also the character of Satan the knowledge of evil. From nature, which now revealed the knowledge of good and evil, man was continually to receive warning as to the results of sin...In the natural world God has placed in the hands of the children of men the key to unlock the treasure house of His Word. The unseen is illustrated by the seen; divine wisdom, eternal truth, infinite grace, are understood by the things that God has made.

"Children should be encouraged to search out in nature the objects that illustrate Bible teachings, and to trace in the Bible similitudes drawn from nature."

*Child Guidance* 47 – "Only in the light that shines from Calvary can nature's teaching be read aright."

*Child Guidance* 48-49 – "Educate the children and youth to consider the works of the great Master Artist, and to imitate the attractive graces of nature in their character building."

*Child Guidance* 50 – "The contemplation and study of God's character as revealed in His created works will open a field of thought that will draw the mind away from the low, debasing, enervating amusements. The knowledge of god's works and ways we can only begin to obtain in this world; the study will be continued throughout eternity.

"His [Jesus'] education was gained from Heaven-appointed sources, from useful work, from the study of the Scriptures, from nature, and from the experiences of life—God's lesson books, full of instruction to all who bring to them the willing hand, the seeing eye, and the understanding heart.

"And spread out before Him was the great library of God's created works. He who had made all things studied the lessons which His own hand had written in earth and sea and sky. Apart from the unholy ways of the world, He gathered stores of scientific knowledge from nature. He studied the life of plants and animals and the life of man. From His earliest years He was possessed of one purpose; He lived to bless others. Fro this He found resources in nature; new ideas of ways and means flashed into His mind as He studied plant life and animal life....

"Thus to Jesus the significance of the Word and the works of God was unfolded, as He was trying to understand the reason of things.

Heavenly beings were His attendants, and the culture of holy thought and communings was His. From the first dawning of intelligence He was constantly growing in spiritual grace and knowledge of truth.

"Every child may gain knowledge as Jesus did. As we try to become acquainted with our heavenly Father through His Word, angels will draw near, our minds will be strengthened, our characters will be elevated and refined."

*Sons and Daughters of God* 241 – "There is need of a close study of nature under the guidance of the Holy Spirit. The Lord is giving object lessons. He is making holy truths familiar to the human mind, through the most simple things of nature."

*Messages to Young People* 253 – "If the young would study the glorious works of God in nature, and His majesty and power as revealed in His word, they would come from every such exercise with faculties quickened and elevated. A vigor would be received, having no kin to arrogance."

*Education* 134 – "Only under the direction of the Omniscient One shall we, in the study of His works, be enabled to think His thoughts after Him."

*Education* 133 – "He who studies most deeply into the mysteries of nature will realize most fully his own ignorance and weakness. He will realize that there are depths and heights which he cannot reach, secrets which he cannot penetrate, vast fields of truth lying before him unentered. He will be ready to say, with Newton, 'I seem to myself to have been like a child on the sea-shore finding pebbles and shells, while the great ocean of truth lay undiscovered before me.'"

Study most deeply into the mysteries of nature.

"The book of nature is a great lesson book, which in connection with the Scriptures we are to use in teaching others of His character, and guiding lost sheep back to the fold of God."

# Gardening Sheet

**Lesson** _One_    **Subject** _Nature_

**Title** _"What is Nature?"_

## In Season

Remember, nature is God's thoughts made visible. Cooperate with Him by praying for wisdom to lay out your gardens in a beautiful plan that will bring honor to His name. If you <u>plan</u> to plant plenty of vegetables and flowers you can take bouquets and baskets of love to the elderly and needy.

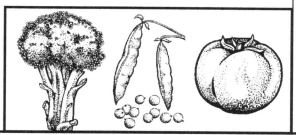

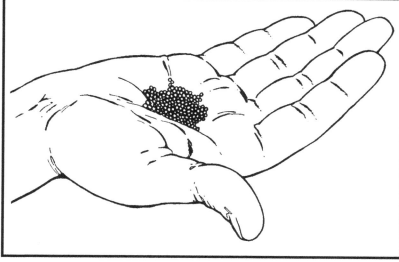

## Out of Season

Plan to start bedding plants during the early spring to be ready when planting time comes. When planning your garden ahead of time you can save much money and be prepared. Use seeds that are not hybrids so you can save your seeds next fall. You will need to study how to save them in the proper way.

Go to the internet to find seed companies whose seeds are not hybrids then you can purchase good seeds. After your first crop you may begin saving your seeds.

# Student Section

"I meditate on all thy works;
I muse on the work of thy hands."
Psalm 143:5

# What Is Nature?

## Research
## God's First Book

The Word of God is the highest and most perfect educational book in our world today. Like a towering rock that fronts the sea, its granite wall is forever receiving the onslaught of the waves. One moment, the waters strike and break in forceless spray upon its fending sides; the next, the sunbeams touch and transfigure the old water-washed gray rock with diamond gleams of light. Thus, with radiant and unbroken front, the word has stood the attacks of ages, and today this mighty citadel of truth remains impregnable as ever.

However, the Scriptures are not God's first book, there was a book even before the Bible. God's first book was the Book of Nature written in the six days of creation; while the second book, the Bible, was written over many hundreds of years by His servants the prophets. *"For the prophecy came not in old time by the will of man: but holy men of God spake as they were moved by the Holy Ghost"* (II Peter 1:21). The first book is a living picture book reflecting the character of God, while the second book is a book of precious words telling about God's character.

Adam and Eve only studied from the Book of Nature, and they were taught by their Maker Himself. He showed them how to read the marvelous pages learning about God's **love** and law. Adam and Eve enjoyed their homeschool and **loved** to attend His classes.

The Book of Nature was written so large that it was illustrated throughout the whole universe. One main feature of this book is the laws that govern this earth, *"**Love** is the fulfilling of the law"* (Romans 13:10).

Today we must study the Bible to understand what God originally wrote on the pages of nature. Then the Holy Spirit can help us understand the words of God, and nature.

> # Nature
> is the garments
> of God;
> Scripture
> is the thoughts
> of God.

Even today much can be learned from God's first book. Read the poem, "What I **Love**," and the story, "A Naturalist's Boyhood Home."

# What I Love

I **love** to rise at break of morn,
    And wander o'er the fertile plains,
When warblers sweet proclaim the dawn,
    And fill the air with joyful strains.

I **love** to view the limpid stream,
    As it meanders gently by,
When sunset with a lingering beam,
    And golden tinge illumines the sky.

I **love** the balmy air of eve,
    With dewy tears and zephyr sighs;
It doth the ruffled mind relieve,
    And soothe the spirit ere it flies.

I **love** the glorious orb of day,
    That gives a sunshine to the heart,
With radiance gilds life's dreary way,
    And sheds on all an equal part.

I **love** the bud and blooming rose
    Whose grace and fragrance give delight;
The violet that humbly grows,
    That wins the sense, and charms the sight.

I **love**, o'er all, fair Nature's Sire
    Who made the earth, the sea, the sky,
The Architect whom all admire,
    The God Supreme who dwells on high.

# A Naturalist's Boyhood Home

John Muir was one of our greatest naturalists.* He loved "Nature's wild gladness." He was born in Scotland in the days when teachers made much use of the rod, for they believed "that there was a close connection between the skin and the memory." His early Scotch training was so strict that by the time he was eleven years old, it is said that he could "recite the New Testament from the beginning of Matthew to the end of Revelation."

When John was eleven years old the family came to America. There were the father and mother and six children. David was the brother next younger than John. The family settled on a farm in "that glorious Wisconsin wilderness." Here John had to work hard, and although his holidays were rare, he still found time to rejoice with the gladness of nature.

John Muir has written many interesting stories about nature. In today's story he takes you on a trip to his boyhood home in Wisconsin. As you go with him into this new, unsettled country, he will share with you some of his boyhood joys in the "grand sunny woods."

---

We enjoyed the strange ten-mile ride through the woods very much. We wondered how the great oxen could be so strong and wise and tame as to pull so heavy a load with no other harness than a chain and a crooked piece of wood on their necks, and how they could sway so obediently to right and left past roadside trees and stumps when the driver said "haw"* and "gee."*

At Mr. Gray's house, father left us for a few days, to build a shanty on the quarter section* he had selected four or five miles to the westward. In the meanwhile, we enjoyed our freedom as usual, wandering in the fields and meadows, looking at the trees and flowers, snakes and birds and squirrels.

With the help of the nearest neighbors the little shanty was built in less than a day after the rough bur-oak logs for the walls and the white-oak boards for the floor and roof were got together. To this charming hut, in the sunny woods, overlooking a flowery glacier meadow and a lake rimmed with white water lilies, we were hauled by an ox team across trackless carex* swamps and low, rolling hills sparsely* dotted with round-headed oaks.

Just at the shanty, before we had time to look at it or the scenery about it, David and I jumped down in a hurry off the load of household goods, for we had discovered a blue jay's nest, and in a minute or so we were up the tree beside it, feasting our eyes on the beautiful green eggs and beautiful birds—our first memorable discovery. The handsome birds had not seen Scotch boys before, and made a desperate screaming as if we were robbers like themselves. We left the eggs untouched, feeling that we were already beginning to get rich, and wondering how many more nests we should find in the grand sunny woods.

Then we ran along the brow of the hill that the shanty stood on, and down to the meadow, searching the trees and grass tufts and bushes, and soon discovered a bluebird's and a woodpecker's nest, and began an acquaintance with the frogs and snakes and turtles in the creeks and springs.

This sudden splash into pure wilderness—baptism in Nature's warm heart—how utterly happy it made us! Nature streaming into us, wooingly teaching her wonderful, glowing lessons, so unlike the dismal grammar ashes and cinders so long thrashed into us. Here without knowing it, we still were at school; every wild lesson a **love** lesson, not whipped but charmed into us. Oh, that glorious Wisconsin wilderness! Everything new and pure in the very prime* of the spring, when Nature's pulses were beating highest, and mysteriously keeping time with our own! Young hearts, young leaves, flowers, animals, the winds and the streams and the sparkling lake, all wildly, gladly rejoicing together!

We soon found many more nests belonging to birds that were not half so suspicious.

Next morning, when we climbed to the precious jay nest to take another admiring look at the eggs, we found it empty. Not a shell fragment was lost, and we wondered how in the world the birds were able to carry off their thin-shelled eggs either in their bills or in their feet without breaking them, and how they could be kept warm while a new nest was being built. Well, I am still asking these questions. I don't know to this day—an example of the many puzzling problems presented to the naturalist.

We soon found many more nests belonging to birds that were not half so suspicious. The handsome and notorious blue jay plunders the nests of other birds, and of course he could not trust us. Almost all the others—brown thrushes, bluebirds, song sparrows, kingbirds, hen hawks, nighthawks, whippoorwills, and woodpeckers—simply tried to avoid being seen, to draw or drive us away, or paid no attention.

We used to wonder how the woodpeckers could bore holes so perfectly round, true mathematical circles. We ourselves could not

have done it even with gouges*
and chisels. We loved to watch
them feeding their young, and
wondered how they could glean
food enough for so many clamor-
ous, hungry, unsatisfiable babies,
and how they managed to give
each one its share; for after the
young grew strong, one would get
his head out of the door hole and
try to hold possession of it to meet
the food-laden parents. How hard
they worked to support their fami-
lies, especially the red-headed and
speckled woodpeckers and flickers;
hammering on scaly bark and de-
caying trunks and branches from
dawn to dark, coming and going at
intervals of a few minutes all the
livelong day!

We discovered a hen
hawk's nest on the top of a tall
oak thirty or forty rods from the
shanty, and approached it cau-
tiously. One of the pair always
kept watch, soaring in wide
circles high above the tree, and
when we tried to climb it, the
big dangerous-looking bird
swooped down at us and drove
us away.

We used to wonder how the woodpeckers could bore holes so perfectly round, true mathematical circles.

We greatly admired the
plucky kingbird, that handsome
little chattering flycatcher that
whips all the other birds. He was
particularly angry when plunder-
ing jays and hawks came near his
home, and took pains to thrash
them not only away from the next
tree but out of the neighborhood.
The nest was usually built on a bur
oak near a meadow where insects
were abundant, and where no un-
desirable visitor could approach
without being discovered.

We greatly admired the plucky kingbird.

When the hen hawk was in sight, the male kingbird immediately set off after him, and it was ridiculous to see that great, strong bird hurrying away as fast as his clumsy wings would carry him, as soon as he saw the little, waspish kingbird coming. But the kingbird easily overtook him, flew just a few feet above him, and with a lot of chattering, scolding notes kept diving and striking him on the back of the head until tired. Then he alighted to rest of the hawk's broad shoulders, still scolding and chattering as he rode along, like an angry boy pouring out vials of wrath. Then, up and at him again with his sharp bill; and after he had thus driven and ridden his big enemy a mile or so from the nest, he went home to his mate, chuckling and bragging as if trying to tell her what a wonderful fellow he was.

The first spring, while some of the birds were still building their nests and very few young ones had yet tried to fly, father hired a Yankee* to assist in clearing eight or ten acres of the best ground for a field. We found new wonders every day, and often had to call on this Yankee to solve puzzling questions. We asked him one day if there was any bird in America that the kingbird couldn't whip. What about the sandhill crane? Could he whip that long-legged, long-billed fellow?

"A crane never goes near kingbirds' nests or notices so small a bird," he said, "and therefore there could be no fighting between them." So we hastily concluded that our hero could whip every bird in the country except perhaps the sandhill crane.

We never tired of listening to the wonderful whippoorwill. One came every night about dusk and sat on a log about twenty or thirty feet from our cabin door and began shouting, "Whip-poor-Will! Whip-poor-Will!" with loud, emphatic earnestness.

"What's that? What's that?" we cried when this startling visitor first announced himself. "What do you call it?"

"Why, he's telling you his name and what he wants you to do," said the Yankee. "Don't you hear it? He says his name is 'Poor Will,' and he wants you to whip him; and you may if you are able to catch him." "Poor Will" seemed the most wonderful of all the strange creatures we had seen. What a wild, strong, bold voice he had, unlike any other we had ever heard on sea or land!

A near relative, the bullbat, or nighthawk, seemed hardly less wonderful. Toward evening, scattered flocks kept the sky lively as they circled around on their long wings a hundred feet or more above the ground, hunting moths and beetles, interrupting their rather slow but strong, regular wing beats at short intervals with quick, quivering strokes while uttering keen, squeaky cries something like "Pfee! pfee!" and every now and then diving nearly to the ground with a loud ripping, bellowing sound, like a bull roaring, suggesting its name; then turning and gliding swiftly up again.

These fine wild gray birds, about the size of a pigeon, lay their two eggs on bare ground without anything like a nest or even a concealing bush or grass tuft. Nevertheless they are not easily seen, for they are colored like the ground. While sitting on their eggs, they depend so much upon not being noticed that if you are walking rapidly ahead they allow you to step within an inch or two of them without flinching. But if they see by your looks that you have discovered them, they leave their eggs or young, and, like a good many other birds, pretend that they are sorely wounded, fluttering and rolling over on the ground and gasping as if dying, to draw you away. When we pursued them, we were surprised to find that just when we were on the point of overtaking them they were always able to flutter a few yards farther, until they had led us about a quarter of a mile from the nest. Then, suddenly getting well, they quietly flew by a roundabout way to their precious babies or eggs.

The songs of the frogs seemed hardly less wonderful than those of the birds, their musical notes varying from the sweet, tranquil* peeping and purring of the hylas* to the awfully deep low-bass bellowing of the bullfrogs. Some of the smaller species have wonderfully clear, sharp voices, and told us their good Bible names in musical tones about as plainly as the whippoorwill. "Isaac, Isaac! Yacob, Yacob! Israel, Israel!" shouted in sharp, ringing, far-reaching tones, as if they had all been to school and severely drilled in elocution.* In the still, warm evenings, big bunchy bullfrogs bellowed, "Skunk! Skunk! Look around! Look around!" and early in the spring, countless thousands of the commonest species, up to the throat in cold water, sang in concert making a mass of music—such as it was—loud enough to be heard at a distance of more than a half a mile.

The songs of the frogs
seemed hardly less wonderful than those of the birds.

# Review
## Place I - II - III

1. In the story there are a number of words that have an asterisk (*) after them. Use a dictionary and define each one.

_____

_____

_____

_____

_____

_____

_____

2 Match the name of the bird in the first list with what the boys found out about each one.

| Name | Found Out |
|---|---|
| Blue jay | 1. Lays eggs on bare ground without nest |
| | 2. One bird always on guard—never allowed boys to approach nest |
| Woodpecker | 3. In some mysterious way took eggs from nest because boys looked at them |
| Hen hawk | 4. Says his own name in song |
| | 5. Had to work very hard digging and hammering to feed family |
| Kingbird | 6. Chased the hen hawk for a mile |
| | 7. Pretends injury to lure boys from nest |
| Whippoorwill | 8. Lays green eggs |
| | 9. Catches insects on the wing |
| Bullbat | 10. Plunders nests of other birds |

3. What was the first book God wrote? What is the difference between His two books? _____

_____

_____

_____

# Research
## Wonderful Works

Nature is all the *"wonderful works"* of God (Psalm 40:5). In the beginning, God was revealed in all the works of creation. It was Christ that spread the heavens, and laid the foundations of the earth. It was His hand that hung the worlds in space, and fashioned the flowers of the field. *"His strength setteth fast the mountains." "The sea is his, and he made it"* (Psalm 65:6; 95:5). It was He that filled the earth with beauty, and the air with song. And upon all things in earth, and air, and sky, He wrote the message of the Father's **love**.

God created nature to attract and interest the minds of His children. He designed the lovely things of the natural world to *"declare the glory of God,"* which is His beautiful character of infinite **love** (Psalm 19:1). *"He hath made his wonderful works to be remembered"* (Psalm 111:4).

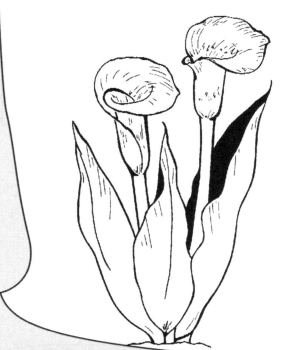

Yes, God's created works are like a big book. Upon every page of this volume may still be traced God's handwriting written in a universal language which all may learn to interpret. The Bible is God's thoughts made audible, nature is God's thoughts made visible and Christ is God's thoughts made audible and visible.

# The Adaptation of Nature to the Human Mind

The varieties of nature are adapted to the varieties of the human mind. The shady glen, with its rich foliage and melody of bird and stream, has its perfection of charms for a pure and pensive spirit. The towering Alps, skirted with pines, tipped with snow, and lit up in richest glory by the rising sun, have their Alpine beauty and sublimity, to awaken deep and lofty thoughts and emotions in a soul formed for the grand as well as for the **lovely**.

Nature was created to have some special beauty to attract each individual mind.

**What do you especially enjoy in nature?**

_____

_____

_____

_____

_____

_____

_____

# Understanding Nature

To truly understand the meaning of nature, we must find the thoughts of God which are shown by each created thing. How shall we receive this kind of wisdom? It is not the same as the knowledge of facts which may be gathered by observing the works of God, important as these may be. But *"wisdom is the principal things"* (Proverbs 4:7). And *"the fear of the Lord, that is wisdom; and to depart from evil is understanding"* (Job 28:28). To learn from nature we must first of all invite the presence of the Spirit of God into our minds and humbly claim God's promise, *"if any of you lack wisdom, let him ask of God, that giveth to all men liberally, and upbraideth not; and it shall be given him"* (James 1:5).

Then, as we walk in the light of God's Word, we continually are blessed with spiritual vision. Spiritual vision is the real secret to understanding nature aright. Oh! it is such a thrilling experience to personally hear the Holy Spirit whisper some deep truth about nature to your soul.

"Thou, Lord, hast made me glad through thy work... O Lord, how great are thy works! and thy thoughts are very deep." Psalm 92:4-5

# Before the Fall

Before Adam sinned, his spiritual vision was so clear that he could read the nature of each animal in the Garden of Eden. That is why he was able to score 100% on the test God gave him when the creatures were brought before him *"to see what he would call them"* (Genesis 2:19). The mind of Adam was so in tune with God's mind that he was able to discern the special characteristics that made each animal what it was, and so he spoke the word which best described their unique nature and qualities.

> *"Let this mind be in you, which was also in Christ Jesus."*
> Philippians 2:5

*"And whatsoever Adam called every living creature, that was the name thereof"* (Genesis 2:19). In other words, Adam agreed with God. In his innocent state, Adam's mind itself was but the expression of the Divine Mind. And so, if you want to really understand the deeper meanings of nature, you too, must *"let this mind be in you, which was also in Christ Jesus"* (Philippians 2:5).

Obedience to the Word of God is another requirement to receive wisdom. David mentioned this fact when he wrote, *"I understand more than the ancients, because I keep thy precepts"* (Psalm 119:100).

# After the Fall

When Adam and Eve sinned by believing and following Satan's word instead of God's Word, they lost their spiritual vision. Receiving the mind of Satan makes a person think wrong thoughts about nature. For example, Eve *"saw that the tree* [of knowledge of good and evil] *was good for food, and that it was...a tree to be desired to make one wise"* (Genesis 3:6). But we know that the taking of the fruit from that tree caused her to lose wisdom, rather than gain it. Perhaps you can now understand what serious results misreading nature can have.

Read Isaiah 40:12-14. Men sometimes suppose that they discover new scientific truths; but they cannot teach God anything. Our God is a God of infinite knowledge.

Today nature is still being misread and it is causing people to lose their souls. An example of this would be the way some people "see" evidence for evolution in nature. But this error goes hand in hand with losing faith in God's word.

### Evolution is not true.

It is much easier to misunderstand the book of nature now than it was in the Garden of Eden. Man's powers have been greatly weakened. And where once was written only the character of **love**, now is also written the character of Satan. Without God's Spirit to aid us, the study of nature would be confusing because nature now illustrates the knowledge of good and evil. And this evil side of nature can serve as a warning to us about the results of sin.

## Nature Is a Key

Those who will believe and practice God's Word will learn precious lessons from the Book of Nature. The whole natural world will become an interpreter of holy truths. Nature is the key that unlocks the treasure-house of the Word of God. The same principles are found in the spiritual and natural world. The operations of nature can help us to understand the operations of the Holy Spirit. It can be a wonderful adventure to search out in nature the objects that illustrate Bible teachings, and also to trace in the Bible the parables drawn from nature.

"The works of the Lord are great, sought out of all them that have pleasure therein."
Psalm 111:2

## Reinforce
## Treasure Hunt!

Use the list below and go on a nature treasure hunt. After you have found your treasures answer these questions about each item:

1. What one thing do you notice about _____?

2. What does that remind you about in the Bible?

3. Find a Bible text about each thing.

### List for Place I - II

A seed from a weed
A green leaf
A rock

### List for Place II - III

Above list
A stick for walking
A root
A piece of charcoal

### Read "God's Treasuries."

# God's Treasuries

The palace of the Vatican at Rome is said to contain more than four thousand apartments. Some of them are of such great length that they might be partitioned into ten divisions, and each division would be long enough for the largest assembly that can be audibly addressed by the human voice. The countless halls, chambers, cabinets, chapels and corridors are stored with the world's most rare and costly collections in science, art, and literature, gathered from every age and every land. The traveler who can stay but a little while in this city hurries across the Tiber while the clanging bell of Saint Peter's are calling the subjects of the Holy See to morning prayer. He takes his stand at the foot of the royal staircase, ready to press in the moment permission shall be given. He enters, thinking to inish the task of exploration in a few moments and to spend the remainder of the day in some other quarter of the city.

But he finds that the first apartment he enters is so vast and rich in stores of art and antiquity that the whole day is not sufficient to examine that alone. When the hour for closing the gates comes, he goes back to his lodgings, weary and wondering how he shall ever find time to explore the labyrinthine mazes of the mighty palace in all its thousand-fold apartments, when a whole day is not enough for one. He derives his deepest impression of the worldly riches and power of the Papacy from the vast storehouse in which it has treasured up the gifts, received in many centuries from all kings and people of the earth. People have been drawn to the most beautiful and costly works of art from all quarters of the world to that one vast repository. He stands amazed in contemplation of that awful spiritual sovereignty which once used the scepter of its power over subjects millions in all lands, and tossed the crowns and scepters of the earth from hand to hand in wild sport, as if they were the playthings of childhood. He returns to his home with the feeling that to know what the Papacy was in its pride and power one must see it enthroned in the Cathedral of St. Peter and in the palace of the Vatican.

The universe is the palace in which the infinite God has stored up the works of His hands and the resources of His power. This mighty treasure-house of the Divine Architect has uncounted millions of apartments, extending as wide as the orbs of heaven roll, and as far as the beams of the morning fly. They are filled with infinite treasures of riches and beauty. Our earth, which seems so vast in the eyes of the inhabitants, is one small room in the palace of the great King. Our present life is the first day given us to begin the study of God's wonders here. We have only just entered the vestibule of the mighty temple which the almighty Builder has reared for His own glory. Through this great house of His kingdom His immortal children are free to range in wonder and in worship. It will take the whole of our earthly day only to glance at the riches and glories with which we are surrounded. And we have only to use the present opportunity well to have our minds in formed and delighted every hour. Then, when the evening comes and we are weary with our work, we shall be per-

mitted to pass on through the gateway of death, and spend the endless years of eternity in ranging at leisure through the everlasting halls of our Father's many-mansioned house.

In this world God brings forth from His infinite treasury such wonders of His power as we can best understand. He sets them in order for us to study, that we may see His greatness and exalt His name. And when we have learned this the first lesson well, He will throw open other apartments of His mighty palace, and bid us pass on from world to world, and from age to age, in wonder and in joy.

# Subjects

Jesus studied nature, as is obvious from the many parables He gave. Since He is our example in everything, we want to follow Him by studying in the lessons ahead such subjects as the heavenly bodies, the Earth and its plants and animals, water systems, and rocks and minerals. We will only be able to make a small beginning in studying the works of God. The subject of nature is so broad and deep that its study will be continued throughout eternity. And the redeemed will find in the cross of Christ their **science** and their **song**. Nature has endless lessons to teach us about the self-sacrificing **love** of our precious Saviour.

The person who studies most deeply into the mysteries of nature will realize that there are depths and heights which he cannot reach. There are mysterious secrets which he cannot penetrate and vast fields of truth lying before him unentered. Well may he say with Newton, "I seem to myself to have been like a child on the seashore finding pebbles and shells, while the great ocean of truth lay undiscovered before me."

May God richly bless you, dear student of the higher school, as you *"meditate on all* [His]... *works"* (Psalm 143:5).

"Ask now the beasts and they shall teach thee; and the fowls of the air, and they shall tell thee: Or speak to the earth, and it shall teach thee: and the fishes of the sea shall declare unto thee."
Job 12:7-8

## Reinforce

Read the poem, "God's Thoughts," and the story, "God Seen in All His Works." Teacher, dictate the spelling words.

# Review
## Place I

1. Do the sheet entitled, "What Is Nature?" Color the words and pictures.

### Place II - III

2. What was the first book God wrote? Describe it.

3. What is nature?

4. Do you think God can help you understand nature?

5. How can we understand nature?

6. What did Adam and Eve lose when they sinned?

7. What does nature unlock?

8. What did Jesus study?

9. Finish this sentence. "Nature has _____ _____ to _____ us about the self-sacrificing _____ of our precious Saviour."

# God's Thoughts

God has a thought for the maple;
Lo, there is the thought—the tree.
What is God's thought for the granite?
Look at the granite, and see.

What God thinks of the grass
Is told by the cool, green sod;
The rose, unfolding its petals,
discloses a thought of God.

His thought for the butterfly
Is writ on the insect's wings;
The word He speaks to the skylark
You hear when it soars and sings.

We think we are more than the flower,
More than the tree or sod;
But ah! do we live our lives
As true to the thought of God?

—*D.M. Henderson*

# What Is Nature?

NATURE IS ALL THE "WONDERFUL WORKS" OF GOD.

# "God Seen in All His Works"

About one hundred and forty years ago in that beautiful part of Germany which borders on the Rhine, there was a noble castle, which, as one traveled on the western banks of the river, could be seen lifting its ancient towers on the opposite side, above the grove of trees about as old as itself.

In that castle there lived a noble gentleman whom we shall call Baron. The baron had only one son who was not only a comfort to his father, but a blessing to all who lived on his father's land.

It happened that, one day while the son was gone, a French gentleman came to see the baron. As soon as this gentleman came into the castle he began to speak of his Heavenly Father in words that chilled the old man's blood. The baron reproved the irreverent speech of the Frenchman saying, "Are you not afraid of offending God, who reigns above, by speaking in such a manner?"

The gentleman said he knew nothing about God, for he had never seen Him. The baron did not reply to what the man said at that time, but the next morning he took him about his **lovely** castle grounds. Next he showed him a very beautiful picture that hung upon the wall inside the castle. The gentleman admired the picture very much, and said, "Whoever drew this picture knows very well how to use his pencil."

"My son drew that picture," said the baron.

"Then your son is a very clever man," said the gentleman.

The baron went with the gentleman into the garden and showed him many beautiful flowers and plantations of forest trees.

"Who has the ordering of this garden?" asked the gentleman.

"My son," replied the baron, "he knows every plant, I may say from the cedar of Lebanon to the hyssop upon the wall."

"Indeed!" said the gentleman, "I shall think very highly of him soon."

The baron then took him into the village and showed him a small neat cottage, where his son had established a school, and where he caused all young children, who had lost their parents, to be received and nourished at his own expense. The children and the gentleman were very much pleased, and when he returned to the castle he said to the baron:

"What a happy man you are to have so good a son!"

"How do you know I have so good a son?"

"Because I have seen his works, and I know that he must be good and clever if he has done all that you have showed me."

"But you have never seen him."

"No, but I know him very well, because I judge of him by his works."

"True," replied the baron, "and this is the way I judge the character of our Heavenly Father. I know from His works that He is a being of infinite wisdom and power and **love**."

The Frenchman felt the force of the reproof, and was careful not to offend the good baron any more by his speech.

# There Is a God

"There is a God," all nature cries—
The earth, the sea, the lofty skies.
The lowliest plant that decks the vale,
The insect sporting on the gale,
The earliest flower that spring gives birth
To adorn and beautify the earth,
The streamlet gliding through the plain,
The wild bird's sweet and plaintive strain,
The blue depths of the boundless sea,
Type of His own immensity.
The sun advancing to the west,
The full moon rising in the east,
The brightly twinkling star of even,
The lightning's flash, the thunder's roar,
They all the Almighty's power adore,
And with united voice proclaim
Through the whole earth, Jehovah's name.
—*Unknown*

# Mark Your Bible

## Nature

**1. Nature is all the "wonderful works" of God.**

**Psalm 40:5** – *"Many, O Lord my God, are thy wonderful works which thou hast done, and thy thoughts which are to usward: they cannot be reckoned up in order unto thee: if I would declare and speak of them, they are more than can be numbered."*

**2. Did God plan for His people to study nature?**

**Matthew 6:28** – *"Consider* [carefully observe] *the lilies of the field, how they grow."*

**3. Can we always understand nature at first glance?**

**Psalm 143:5** – *"I meditate on all thy works; I muse on the work of thy hands."*

**4. God created nature to make man happy and increase his wisdom.**

**Psalm 92:4-6** – *"For thou, Lord, hast made me glad through thy work: I will triumph in the works of thy hands. O Lord, how great are thy works! and thy thoughts are very deep. A brutish man knoweth not; neither doth a fool understand this."*

**5. To the discerning heart, nature reveals the wisdom, power, and love of God.**

**Psalm 104:24** – *"O Lord, how manifold are thy works! in wisdom hast thou made them all: the earth is full of thy riches."*

# Remind

1. Look at all the books in your home library and think how many more volumes there are in nature.

2. When unlocking the door of the house for father remember nature is the key that unlocks the treasure-house of the Word of God.

3. Look at pictures of the ocean or visit the ocean—consider what Newton said, there is a "great ocean of truth laying undiscovered before me."

Some material adapted from the following books: *A Cyclopaedia of Nature Teachings, Our Father's House,* and *True Education Reader*.

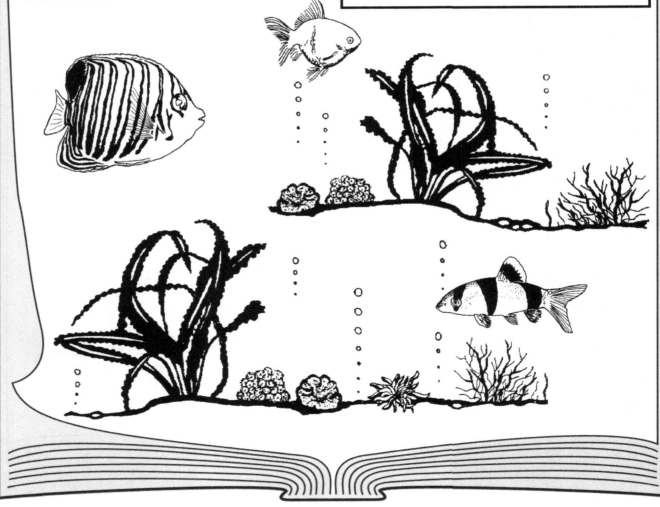

# Reinforce

1. Visit a library and notice how many volumes there are in the section for nature. Plan to study one page of the Book of Nature each day.

2. As you look at a picture book think how God's 3-D picture book, "nature," has limitless and more interesting pages. Keep a nature journal.

3. Learning how to read nature's pages:

• take a picture of nature

• study it carefully

• turn it over and recall what you saw

• look at the picture and notice all you might have missed

• now find one object in nature (such as a tree) and repeat the process. Study the object carefully. Then without looking at it further list all the interesting things you observe about it.

• Study more about the item you found in nature from resource books.

• Study about the item from Scripture. Write down at least one spiritual lesson that you have learned.

• Go back and observe the item and recall how it teaches you about God.

# Ruminate

Since God is the source of all true knowledge,
it is, as we have seen, the first object of education
to direct our minds to His own revelation of Himself.
Adam and Eve received knowledge through
direct communion with God;
and they learned of Him through His works.
All created things, in their original perfection,
were an expression of the thought of God.
To Adam and Eve nature was teeming
with divine wisdom. But by transgression
man was cut off from learning
of God through direct communion and,
to a great degree, through His works.
The earth, marred and defiled by sin,
reflects, but dimly the Creator's glory.
It is true that His object lessons
are not obliterated.
Upon every page of the great volume
of His created works
may still be traced His handwriting.
Nature still speaks of her Creator.
Yet these revelations are partial and imperfect.
And in our fallen state, with weakened powers
and restricted vision, we are incapable
of interpreting aright.
We need the fuller revelation
of Himself that God has given
in His written word."

—*Education 16-17*

# Outline of School Program

| Age | Grade | Program |
|---|---|---|
| Birth through Age 7 | Babies Kindergarten and Pre-school | *Family Bible Lessons* (This includes: Bible, Science–Nature, and Character) |
| Age 8 | First Grade | *Family Bible Lessons* (This includes: Bible, Science–Nature, and Character) + Language Program (*Writing and Spelling Road to Reading and Thinking* [WSRRT]) |
| Age 9-14 or 15 | Second through Eighth Grade | *The Desire of all Nations* (This includes: Health, Mathematics, Music, Science–Nature, History/Geography/Prophecy, Language, and Voice–Speech) + Continue using WSRRT |
| Ages 15 or 16-19 | Ninth through Twelfth Grade | 9 – *Cross and Its Shadow I*\* + Appropriate Academic Books<br><br>10 – *Cross and Its Shadow II*\* + Appropriate Academic Books<br><br>11 – *Daniel the Prophet*\* + Appropriate Academic Books<br><br>12 – *The Seer of Patmos*\* (Revelation) + Appropriate Academic Books<br><br>\*or you could continue using *The Desire of Ages* |
| Ages 20-25 | College | Apprenticeship |

Made in the USA
Las Vegas, NV
17 September 2021